EVERYBODY

EVERYBODY

POEMS BY

ALBERT GOLDBARTH

LynxHousePress

Spokane, Washington

Published by Lynx House Press, Spokane, Washington
Copyright © 2022 by Albert Goldbarth
Printed in the United States of America

Book and jacket design by Jodi Miller-Hunter
Cover art by Skyler Lovelace
Cover background photo by Kees Scherer
Author Photo by Michael Pointer

FIRST EDITION

Cataloging-in-Publication Data is available from the Library of
Congress.
ISBN 978-0-89924-184-5

Everybody's got a hungry heart.

– Bruce Springsteen

for Skyler

Without her there would have been less of myself.

– Mika Waltari, *The Egyptian*

Contents

"EVERYBODY ELSE OUT THERE" IS TOO MANY FOR US TO IMAGINE

["The portraits of saints...."]	15
Urologist's Finger	16
Succulent Haunches, Etc.	19
Amount	21
John Keats's Hair	23
Separate	25
Impossible Flying	27
Moon Song	29
A Matter of Scale	32
Golden Moment	36
The Sky and the Skies	38
Mingles	42

SHORT STORIES

["Ah! The promise of an opening line!"]	49
Terrible, Unfair Burdens	50
A.M. Shift	51
Mr. And Mrs. Music Critic	52
The Problem with Mystic Wisdom	53
Second-Hand Effects	54
Portrait in Three Liquid Stages	55
Patient	56
Needed	57
Resists	58
My Most Horrible Thought for Today	59
Night	60
["The grasses bend"]	61
Pane of Glass	62
1931	63
Their Expert Work	64
["The church bell tolls"]	65

The Barn and Its Shadow   66
The Joke About Stephen Hawking   67
A Poem   68
["But the bed didn't want them in it,"]   69
Stories   70
["You woke, so you stopped dreaming."]   71
Men   72
["I know a secret about the world."]   73
Direction   74
Neighbor   75
["Overhead,"]   76
Funeral Service   77
Tundra   78
The Mine   79
To Every Time of Day, Its Physics   80

LESS

Small Suite   85
Less   99
Betweenish   103

"Everybody Else Out There" is Too Many for Us to Imagine

The portraits of saints in this medieval cathedral...the painter has given them, for all of the garish insignia of their martyrdom, expressions of bland indifference.

Perhaps his talent didn't extend to facial nuance, or perhaps he mistakenly thought this passed for a kind of ascendancy out of the realm of mere human affairs. The final effect, however, is a row of bored accountants at a staff meeting.

One is exhibiting the wheel she was (or is about to be?) tortured on. It's fiendishly spiked. It's carnival colored—canary, aqua, oxblood—like the wheel of a gypsy caravan wagon. It's saying its favorite axle lubrication is human blood.

One is filled with arrows. *Filled.* One has the jaws of two enormous wild boars inextricably fastened onto his body, sawtooth clamps that foam.

My favorite bears a wound on his side like a great raw T-bone steak that's been attached there.

And yet for all of what we make out in his face, that wound may as well be out of sight beneath a three-piece business suit, invisible to your stare and mine

—the way, the therapist knows, the wound almost always is, for all of us.

Urologist's Finger

In 1930 Izey played a cannibal
for the Lucky Five-Star Circus Caravan,
shaking the bars of his cage with a ferocity
so palpable, the rubes would think if he couldn't
break the bars, his rage would melt them;
and by 1940—having managed to *not* drink
all of his Five-Star salary into oblivion—he
was proudly posing for ads for his company, Isaiah's
Rock Solid Construction, next to the slowly rotating
drum the cement was mixed in (bigger
even than the flame-red midget circus car they crammed
with fifteen clowns and a tiara'd and tutu'd
wiener dog); you can notice him gently
placing his right hand's fingertips
against that great rotundity of industrial metal
with something like the careful touch
of a nurse's fingers feeling for the neck pulse
of a newborn in the preemie ward. Somebody's

the nurse. Somebody's the nurse and she's also
the Duncan Yo-Yo Company yo-yo lady
every-other weekend, astounding the crowds
with Shoot the Moon, with Whoops-a-Daisy.
Somebody deftly trains the wiener dogs ("Delilah Delite
and her Dachsunds!") and somebody else (in fact
the lady clown, Niobe) sews
their tutus, with a nimble exactness, even
when she's heartsore that her daughter in Albuquerque
won't reply to birthday and holiday cards, plus
green-bile pissed at how Joey the Fat Clown
("Mr. Handsy," say the ladies) takes his groping advantage
of her butt when they cram in the midget car.
And so this poem isn't really—or anyway, solely—

about Isaiah, no, except to the extent that it's
about the human genome—its unlimited and flexible
creations, of which you're one, I'm one, and
"everybody else out there" is too many for us to imagine.
Somebody's stitching a spiral of tiny lacquered seeds
upon the breast-cloth that the temple virgins will tie
around the polished wood neck of the goddess. Somebody's
eviscerating a ram. (His son has hung it
to bleed in the bucket.) Somebody knows
what the old-time cowpokes meant by "air-tights"
(canned goods). Somebody, once, would walk along
the water's edge—its bluish-gray infinity
on one side and the massive, grim-lipped stone gods
on the other—and say hello to the person nearing her
in the out-loud, living language of what
we now call "Easter Island script": once,
but no longer. It's gone, it's dead
to our comprehension. Somebody's at the steel mill
and the only language *he* knows at the Building 14
bonderizer is eight shit-boring hours
of the single syllable *drone*. Somebody is sitting
in the Buddha's posture. Somebody knows exactly when
the cops patrol his designated seven blocks
of Wabash Street, and his in-the-shadows
livelihood depends on this. There are drugs to sell (and use)
and flesh to sell (and use). Somebody's the cop.
Somebody's feeding the pelicans. It turns out what we are

is a tightly outlined individual self—but
done in watercolor, and so always open to bleeding
across the outline, into the life next door.
It's strange—but then, Creation is strange.
I have no explanations or guidance.
In Albuquerque, a woman has labored—methodically,
penitentially—to forget, to disown, her past; and yet
sometimes when she's alone in her office (*Director*, it says

in gilt lettering on the frosted glass of the office door)
she'll hesitantly remove the double locket
from its satin case, and stare at that goddam circus clown
and cheap-ass faked-up "cannibal" who won't stop
being her parents in her subconscious no matter
how hard her consciousness tries. Somebody
this, and that. I once tried writing a poem I called
"The Adventures of the Urologist's Finger." Somebody
is reading an augury out of the liver
of a freshly slaughtered goat; *his* finger
traces a purple splotch of a sun
above a world of petaled, mazey, liver-color plains.
It's somebody's future.

Succulent Haunches, Etc.

It's hard to relinquish
the Great Chain of Being, for obvious reasons
—that structuring force from a halcyon time
when we were both (illogically, for such a logical system)
the height of Creation *and* its center.
It seemed so sensible: first, some unicellular jelly-being
flagellating its way through First Day ooze; and then
—what? lizards, apes, the whole zoo,
then a shambling creature armed with a club
and a fearful-but-hopeful dream of controlling fire;
and then—*ta-DAAA!*—us,
our decanters of a sweetly ruby port,
our Dickens novels, our penicillin. Sensible.
Maybe if you and I had been alive in the days
of the Great Chain of Being's full flowering
we'd have confidently (and tediously) lectured our guests
—as the port was being poured—
on the wisdom of pillorying that decadent
twizzlehead Darwin. We can banter "quark" and "neutrino"
and the pieties of PETA daylong,
but still, the old, unshakable comforts
—the certainties—refuse to yield up
our lofty status in the Order of Things. Today
in a single hour my driving hauled me past the dancing pig
with the porkpie hat and the succulent haunches,
trotting its hot-pink neon jig
on the roof of The Barbeque Hut; and the hen
that's sledding down the slope of the Chick-Inn Shack
on an outsized silver skillet; and the smiling steer
in its great marshmallowy chef's hat, winking nonstop
at the backed-up traffic in front of Burgeroo...
they're so happy to offer their lesser lives,
if only it will allow our own ongoing

or find us delightedly licking our lips,
so willing to sacrifice themselves
for our well-being, as are
—in case my vegan niece and nephew feel left out—
the do-si-do'ing carrots and tasseled ears of corn
at the local farmers market on Saturday afternoons.
But even in their display of complaisant subservience,
they seem to possess a kind of karmic wisdom we find it
impossible to live by. Take us
inside you, they say. Recombine us inside you.
All that matters isn't matter,
but radiance. Everything came from the stars,
and everything—although you're entitled
to loving your wife, and writing your poems, and voting your vote—
returns there.

Amount

Like everything else: the more it *can* be computed
by the media, the more *(surprise!)* there is to compute.
The number of billionaires under age thirty-five.
The number of bodies heaped in the fields
after the genocide. The decibel level of flies beginning
to settle on those corpses. How many
streakers per year in a mad and naked dash
through public sporting events. The weight, the length,
of gigabytes, of marriages, of satellite junk projected
to plummet from orbit. Let's get specific: 100 billion

neurons in the human brain. Over a quarter-million
birds in the private collection that Lord Walter Rothschild
sold to the American Museum of Natural History
(which also has, by the way, 600,000 jars of fishes
preserved in alcohol). The Hindu *kali yuga*
("age of strife") will last 432,000 years. Big Bill,
a pig that was owned by a Buford Butler
of Jackson, Tennessee in the 1930s, was nine feet long
"and had the amazing weight of 2,552 pounds."
Don't even *start* me on whales. Well...okay, go ahead,

start me. But I don't mean their tonnage, impressive
though that is: the right whale's *testes* alone are a ton
("the size of washing machines"). I mean that the female
births a single calf—not a litter—and everything
she knows of aquatic survival and care is invested
there, 24-7. We can see it—in *its* element—bob
bob bobbin' along as jauntily as the robin in the song,
on a lawn. We can see it cupped in a curl
of the female's flukes with the contentedness of the infant
in a mother-and-child portrait by Mary Cassatt.

I mean in 2018 the newborn calf of the whale
Tahlequah died just after birth,
and for seventeen days she was witnessed using her snout
to push its carcass around the cobalt waters
off Washington State. "Amount," I titled this,
but any idea of measurement seems inadequate
next to grief like that. And yes, we shouldn't
too readily ascribe our human emotions to them.
But...seventeen days. Loving it still,
in death as in life, one gentle thud at a time.

John Keats's Hair

Enter the model, Lacey, who matter-of-factly
and in thirty seconds disrobes (the verb is literal:
a terrycloth robe cascades to the floor
in a single pink pour, and she kicks it out of sight),
and then for three exacting hours she's a column
of skin the light turns into various faceted vectors
someone captures—or tries to, anyway—in acrylics.
Is anything more naked? Well, yes, if she's

a true professional, and mentally floats away
throughout this process she's accustomed to for years now.
Easy-peasy. But revealing her dreams
in her therapist's office—reluctantly cupping
her hands inside her mind, and then lifting them
out now into the clinical light muck-full
with the dark, embarrassing adventures of a self
beyond the strictures of her conscious control

...that's naked. As you would feel, too,
asquirm in that chair, for that long hour,
as completely skinned as an apple can be skinned,
set on the counter for the air to go to work at.
Speaking of peeling: the ethical question
a science article raises: 3,000 years
in the future (that is, today) do mummies
have a right to privacy? We imagine them

being unspooled from their resin-slathered bandaging
in a cartoonish ecdysiast way and then exhibited
under the naked museum light to the naked
gazes that we pay at the door to carry inside, but really
it's so much more invasive: X-rays,
gas chromatography/mass spectrometry,

etc. Toxicologist Svetlana Balabanova
has chemically broken in to the hair remains

of mummies from Peru and Egypt and found there,
she claims, evidence of cocaine and THC.
You: would you call this exciting scientific discovery
...or violation? I'm flipping a coin. We know
John Keats's opium addiction
from a lock of his hair. We know Elizabeth Bishop's
poems and Nabokov's notes for a novel
that neither elected to publish while alive,

although they're published now, as firmly pinned
and catalogued for our scrutiny as the butterflies
he caught and placed in cases—wings
as delicate as the breath we'd see
if satin breathed, and splayed out
like a sample of skin from a rainbow.
Preemie ward / the morgue / the strip club /
drone above your backyard tanning / heat-capture

technology...naked naked naked naked.
One Sunday Lacey's boyfriend picks her up
from police HQ on a bitter winter night
when the air in your nostrils crackles. The cops had wanted
to question her. They'd snipped some hair for analysis.
Bundled up in two sweaters, mittens, a scarf,
and a down-lined Persian lamb's-wool coat,
she's never felt so exposed.

Separate

*April 12, 1961: The Russian Yuri Gagarin became "the first
person ever to ride a rocket into space.... He was able to
parachute out at an altitude of 23,000 feet [and]...floated
down from the sky to land in a freshly plowed field."*
— *50 Greatest Moments of the Space Age*

This couple—I'm going to say age sixty,
married over forty years, and callused
as thick as pigskin on their palms from half a century
of day-long manual farm work—still
caress each other at bedtime with the delicacy
of care (is "care" where "caress" comes from?)
we associate with a petal-thin baby-skin touch.
At night their heads on their pillows are so close
that an eighth-inch static electric spark
could bridge their hair, and it sometimes seems
a dream might travel back and forth
across that tiny flyway, so swiftly
and frequently, we'd lose track of exactly whose
subconscious was its origin. And even so,

yes even so, why *does* she [here, you'll have to fill in
some great exasperating female illogic] and
why, in the name of Jesu Christ and the Commissar's ass
(they're Russian, these two farmland proles), oh *why*
does he [add here, a lunkhead inanity, some
dead-end dunderwitted scheme that only a man
could conjure up and luster to a sheen].
I join you in disappointment: if even *they*
don't always share a common language, and some
days none at all—these two who have buried
a daughter together, out past the potato rows;
and cursed the Council; and freed the breech-calf
stuck in the mama-cow; and danced in crazy circles

in lightningstorms, together—what hope is there

the "Free World" and "the Reds" will ever chorally
sing an anthem of understanding? The Israelis
and the Palestinians share a species, a genome,
hummus and pita bread, and still would cheerfully toast
the deaths of the others with wine in goblets
fashioned from the skulls of the others [or here insert
your own example: Democrats/Republicans, etc.], so
do we *really* believe the aliens from Galaxy X-Minus
—maybe methane-bodied; chitinous;
seven-brained (or no-brained: "thinking"
without "thought")—are going to speak with us
in comity? Our crime statistics—white on white;
black on black; North Side gang on South Side—
aren't encouraging. Still, don't we cherish

this sci-fi trope from the Cold War years:
the aliens attack Earth with their grim X-Minus
death rays, and America and Russia now
join forces in a perfect (and lasting) harmony,
above misapprehension. In the "real world" in 1961,
our couple walks out into the fields, where
they're obviously terrified to see a figure
wafting down from the sky, then landing
thumpingly, then approaching them.
A United States saboteur? A drooling monster?
So to ease their fear, Yuri Gagarin shouts
his soon-to-be-famous announcement: "I am one of yours!"
Which was true. But it was also true
that he was addressing two separate yous.

They cling to each other, but think their own thoughts.

Impossible Flying

*"To make a real hippo fly, you'd have to strap a pair of wings on
it so large that...well, the project is doomed from the start because
the mass of muscle needed to power those gigantic wings would
be too heavy for the wings to lift. If you wanted to make a flying
animal, you wouldn't start with a hippo."*
– *Richard Dawkins*

—Nor a hummingbird 300 feet long,

although one can be found among the famous "Nazca lines"
which are scored in the high, dry landscape
of Peru; the tail alone
of a nearby condor figure fans out 160 feet, accomplished
as a single winding line, as is the monkey,
and the whale, and the rest of this extraordinary bestiary
that's drawn to the scale of gods. Nor would we bet

on the marriage of Elliott and Dana to last,
to lift, to have in any way the feel of being
functionally airborne: not when each of them
is a heavy collection of habits and character
rusted tight, immovable. As evidence:
their nights of fights that well up
with the reek of bile; their days of lame excuses
for his clawed cheek, for her punched-in scrawl of capillaries under
        an eye.
Nothing about such love could slip the granite fist
of gravity.
            And yet...

some experts do believe
those figures on the Nazca plain were made to be procession trails
shamans walked in meditation: focusing
on otherness, and feeling...well, the way the *om* might feel

as it's lost inside the body of a chant
and flies to somewhere unattached
to the corporeal. If supercruiser cargo planes

the size of coliseums can be motes upon the clouds,
why be surprised that the Egyptian goddess
charged with overgoverning the zero-gees ascension
of the sun each dawn is Tau-e-ret, the hippo? And because
the day is born within her tutelage...because

of her rotundity itself, and what it signals as she waddles out
on her two hind legs from her swamp home, to conduct the sunlight's
daily liberation from the hold of the horizon...Tau-e-ret
the hippo is also the goddess of childbirth—the one
who presides in the room (or over the field) where the woman
is coated in labor-sweat, and the spread of her legs
aligns the rest of her musculature and its rhythms
into a chute, and a voice says "push" (in ancient Egyptian),
"push," and she responds with the long sounds of a language
that was old before the seed of Egypt ever was planted,
and *then*, as everything quivers upon the cusp, the name
Tau-e-ret is invoked, and the will of Tau-e-ret is enacted.
Dana says
            that at the moment her water broke,

a handful of her consciousness was let loose, and it floated
near the ceiling of the room, and witnessed. (Such is the power
of natal endorphins.) Elliott watched too: "The whole
next day, guys, I was walking on air!" And whether
their child "saved their marriage," served as an alleviating breath
inside that thick and sour atmosphere...is somewhere
way beyond the proper boundary of this poem.
I'm merely saying in the minute just after the cord was severed,
Elliott helped sponge Dana's face, he vowed to make everything
"right again," and then kneeled to kiss the wings
of blood that had opened on each of her thighs.

Moon Song

To successfully boil a sow's head, so
it infuses the soup with maximum porcine savor
but the face slides off intact enough
to dry and make into a pouch, you must:
[instructions]. To construct a timeline history
of philosophy in which the Western and Eastern traditions
remain independent and yet, when appropriate,
intersect: [instructions]. These things
anchor us, these "pursuits," these "interests," they hammer
our fearful glimmer of mortality into the surface
of what feels like a permanence, they happily distract us, they
allow us to believe "life" *isn't*
a shorthand form for "shelf life." Someone somewhere knows
what "bort" is [*c.f.* "diamonds"]; someone else knows all of the words
to all of the Smoky Mountains fiddle tunes; and someone else
is expert in the Buddha's pendulous earlobes
and the Zoroastrian "burial" where the corpse is set
on a roof and the vultures carry it up to Eternity
peck by peck. To know

what your neighborhood coke connection means
by a "bump," what "footballs" are, or "bars," or "yellows."
To know what the "paternoster" is, and what
(assuming God Himself didn't speak a rousing
King James English) is the language the Bible
was written in. Or simply to know which cream to use
on the eczema in the baby's folds of flesh,
those petals, those [kisskiss] doughy declivities!
These personal worlds implant us, or at least
seem to implant us, in the greater World: we cherish,
necessarily, this seeming. To determine the rate of incidence
per capita of SHC (Spontaneous Human Combustion)
in rural areas: [diagram] [formula] [graph].

To patch the canoe, to walk the red carpet
stylishly and effortlessly, to kick the habit,
to chart the movements of exoplanets (that can't be seen
directly, but can be inferred): [Googlesearch repeatedly].
Because the wheat and the scythe are magnets
attracting each other. Because the wheat and the scythe
are an ancient glyph for "inevitable." To master chess.
To feel the grapes go slush beneath your naked toes.
Because when Mary lifted His lips to her nipple
in the manger, she could already feel exactly how the bones
of the body conformed to the shape of the cross.
Because the wheat and the scythe are an ancient glyph
for "demise." To study African insect communities
in terms of economic structures: [data].
To fuck on that bitch's other baby daddy:
[drama] [gossip] [drama]. Or simply to stare
as a blade-of-a-shadow pares another
hour-of-rind off the face of the sundial
in the yard. Because the geese are a sign:
we can't fly backward, we have to continue,
there's only a forward line. There's only a forward line that,
like the pencil's, only moves ahead
through the pencil's diminishment. And so
in our trembling, our brevity, and our foundering in the winds:
the church box supper, the block of alabaster to sculpt,
the dirt bike, the mosh pit, the terrarium, the model shoot, and so
the voice inside us: *[voiceover] pound me, pound me,*
against time, undeniably into the planet
unless

you're me one day or someone like me,
seventy-four, and learning that your best friend
Michael Cissell just died at forty-five:
he bicycled, he ran, he hiked with his two boys:
dead at forty-five. And then for a while

you *won't* be on this planet in entirety.
A part of you will be floating someplace
not completely physical and not completely
in everyone else's understanding of time.
It's a little like visiting the moon,

the death moon. Yes, you're still in sight
of Earth; you haven't evaporated
into the zero of outer space. But as everyone knows,
you weigh less here. It's still you,
but the breathing is different.
The dark side is only a moon-leap away.
The nearness of the void is different.

A Matter of Scale

1

A high speed chase, and then after the back/forth bullets
lodged in their various destinations, some of them lethally
—a skull, a belly, the small of a back—the cop car sirens
segued into ambulance sirens, and then—as happens
eventually, for a while at least—this segued into silence again;

and the ten-year-old in a doorway, who had watched this drama
stony-eyed, as people doubled over and fell,
was on her knees now
sobbing for a cat caught in the crossfire....

Who's to say our store of love can't be doled out
as illogically as the heartbreak sorrow our gods disperse?

2.

"How amazing is *that!*" I can hear
my old friend Michael exclaiming,
although he's been dead for three years.
But he loved to have a mellowing drink or two
and align his amateur back yard telescope
with whatever that night's designated wonder was
—his capacity for astonishment
untainted by the daily. And indeed,
it *is* amazing,

the NASA rover *Perseverance*
landing on Mars, on time, *en pointe,*
and selfying photos back to Earth
through 35 million miles of void

with the seemingly unthinking ease
of a fashionista letting the world admire
how becoming the red is.
35 million miles!
Mars! *Another planet!* (I channel
the exclamation points from Michael.)
And all of the stats in the *National Geographic*
cover story are also cause
for a goggle-eyed awe:

700,000
(and that's pre-*Perseverance*) images
of that "ruddy" "vermilion" "peach-plum"
"plain old beige" or "salmon pink"
(depending on who your source is)
planetscape, including

Valles Marineris, a canyon
"100 miles wide in places
and nine times longer than Arizona's
Grand Canyon: on Earth it would extend from New York City
to Los Angeles"; and Olympus Mons,
"more than twice the height of Mount Everest,
it's the largest known volcano in the solar system"
—a perfect nexus-spot for gods and mythic beasts,

the Babylonian Nergal ("god of pestilence and war"),
the Persian Pahlavani Sipher,
Tui for the Norse (hence "Tuesday"), Ares
for the Greeks ("the god of battle") and,
most charmingly perhaps, the Aboriginal link
"to Kogolongo, the native red-tailed black cockatoo"
—and perfect, rich dream-hatchery

for our movie madness: *A Message from Mars* (1913);
A Trip to Mars (1918), in which "essentially

the spaceship is a dirigible with wings";
Mars Attacks the World (1938); the ridiculous
Flight to Mars (1951) with Marguerite Chapman
as "the leggiest astro-scientist in the universe";
Monster from Mars (1953), and the next year,
Devil Girl From Mars. All of it,

amazing!
            And yet today, for me,
if I could re-collect and reassemble
Michael's organs—bring them back
through time against the forward grain
of their donation—I believe his body
(five-foot-six, if that) would eclipse, fully,
any planet.

It's always a matter of scale

and context, isn't it?
As an experiment, let me bring back,
for a final time,
the ten-year-old girl from section 1.

Mars, that bloody pustule:
Mars, that flashing ruby spangle:
if we set it
—every canyon, god, and movie—
in the pan I've saved for weighing it
on the balance-pans...

Mars will rise

if the other pan holds a single cat
with its single bullet,
such is the way we subjectively apportion
the things we care about.

3.

And Michael,
a wealth of anecdotal stories suggests
that sometimes...*something*...transfers
from the organ donors along with the physical parts.
    Those people who wake from their surgery
speaking in a language they never knew.
    "I used to *hate* fish. Now I *crave* it!"
    The little scaredy-pants who now loves riding
adrenalin-thumpthump roller coasters, having received
a kidney from a fan of *The Plunge* and *The Boomerang*.
Right now I picture a woman your age

who can breathe due to your émigré lungs.
Her career as an astro-scientist keeps her busy enough
without children; and even so, sometimes
she'll halt now over her formulae or a grant proposal
and hear two voices—faint; one part annoying
and one part deeply loving—in orbit around her mind.
Sometimes she'll take a break in the middle of what
was once a wholly sedentary life, and bike
—the way you used to do with Guthrie and Ro.
And sometimes when the weather permits,
she'll pour herself some Wild Turkey
(is this amazing, or what?) and step out
under the night sky, looking at it the way she did
when she was ten—three decades ago!—
to mingle with the stars overhead,
directly, no computer screen
or logarithms or algorithms intervening,
just her and the stars that call to her
with an intimacy, that enter her
with a wild transfusion of glory.

Golden Moment

*Of the year 1776: "Six states regarded themselves as 'three-sided,' which
meant that their citizens considered their western boundaries
still open until they reached the Pacific Ocean."*
– A.J. Langguth

We know it can't last. Eventually
the fourth wall of the box slams down—just ask
the lab rat. Eventually
the rent comes due; the hourglass
in your spouse's love runs out of sand;
the Big Guys in their Headquarters want
their favor returned; the candidate you voted for,
who won, who *won*, is done with the beginning
honeymoon weeks of the first 100 days;
your body checks its watch and sees it's time
to be a different, lesser body. Even so, that golden
promissory moment, when the vista is unlimited
possibility...! I'm reading about the man

released from death row, after fifteen years,
and after DNA of his reversed the scumsuck work
of a bought-up witness. I think nothing compares
exactly, although it's tempting to imagine
a NASA specialist in bio-dome design
in her yard at night, looking up at the moon,
at a universe backing the moon, where any kind
of habitable wonder might be engineered one day,
beyond the rim of the known. And so with this former

incarceree. His soul was squeezed to the size of a cockroach,
how could it not? While on the outside...
Christmases, fishing trips, good lovin',
this "internet thing" they talk about....

And then one day "it was all a mistake."
A fifteen-year mistake. A cockroach mistake.
He's free to leave, to approach the gates
with a cheap new suit and a hundred dollars.
We know it can't last; but let's applaud

his spontaneous, innocent dance of joy
in the parking lot of a prison in Connecticut
as he faces west, and seems to inhale the bracing,
untouched air above the Rockies; and, beyond it,
the air above the salmon ladders of the northwest
when the falls are thick with those silver, jacking muscles;
and the still air off the coast where a dolphin
nuzzles against a swimmer as if in invitation,
voicing a word...
                    the siren call
of a country that we once thought had no end.

The Sky and the Skies

*As every schoolchild used to know, Benedict Arnold began as a zealous
American loyalist in the Continental Army (suffering a musket ball
wound to his left leg in the Saratoga/Quebec campaign; leading
his men through hellish bouts of starvation and forced marches in
underprovisioned conditions; and facing outsized enemy fire), and so
proving himself to be George Washington's most courageous general...
but later sold his services to the British cause for 6,315 pounds up front
and an annual salary of 650 pounds.*

We call it a brain—the singular. There's
Einstein's brain. My aunt's, that
in my childhood was daily eaten away at
by the cancer, until we pictured it
as a soiled pink-gray lace. The brain
the Egyptian embalmers hooked out through the nose,
before the mummywrap was slathered
in conserving goo and coiled around.
But read about a battle,
or read a witness report
to a local violent crime, and it's so often
like this: "His skull was smashed, and blood and

brains spilled onto the dirt."
The plural. Which may of course
and in fact be more accurate.
There are many of us
in each of us.

The same Mrs. Sodderhock (eighth grade
history, right after lunch) who everyone
adored, who made the girls desire
a better self for themselves, and had the boys

in adolescent dreamydreamy land,
who founded the Volunteer Reading
Advocates Program at the synagogue
and donated blood and saved the whales,

at the end of the second semester was brusquely
marched from school in handcuffs
squeezed between two cops; and while the gossiped
details—*men,* and *money,* and *a gun*—
kept floating around for a month in our thin
eighth-graders' understanding of adult complexities,
what we *knew* was, as she exited the school

we saw her face switch
into another face, a clouded face,
as if a glass of water had been stirred
with sludge from the bottom muck
of a river in somebody else's life.

It's the weakest link—she taught
American history—that has me bringing
Benedict Arnold onstage one more time.
But there were two of him

too. One was that filthy thing,
a traitor...at least, from America's
point of view. *A traitor.* Like
my aunt Regina's brain, that turned
against her, as the body, sadly,
sometimes does. At the funeral home

the family took their comfort in repeating
—as if at the sight of one of the Catholic Church's
"incorruptible saints"—*She looks*

just like herself! Okay. But the very
wonder of that implies she wasn't,
any longer, the self—that is, the *same* self—
that they'd spent her lifetime quarreling with and loving
(those are synonymous in my family).
After every 1960s chemical carpet-bombing and nostrum
had revoked its golden promises...my aunt
was defeated, fatally, by what we used to call
a fifth column—conquered
from inside herself.

The sun is so *spectacularly* gorgeous
in this photograph! An intervening curl of smoke
has loaned it the perfection of a machine-milled circle,
a penny, or a brass token
from a century-past World's Fair,
and has imbued it with a saffron color,
peach [times] peach. Too bad

the caption tells us the smoke is bomb-smoke
from an Israel-Palestine conflict.
So the sky too
has an array of possible faces. Or

we each have an array of different identities
with which to interpret the same one sky.
I've researched some of those girls
that Mrs. Sodderhock inspired, and a few

do seem to be contented, useful to their communities,
raising children of similar kind.
Some others, though.... We all know

that the sky above the Yale graduation party

is also the sky above where the women
prison inmates are being granted an exercise hour
inside a gray stone compound.
What can I say?—like you,
I've tried to be a cohesive entity
day to day, but if *The Lord giveth*
and if *The Lord taketh away*...how fully
uniform can we be, based on that model?

When Benedict Arnold was captured
in Virginia by American troops, his fear
—the sentence for traitors and spies traditionally
was death—he counterbalanced in his hopes
with his well-known charm and general luck.
"What do you imagine my fate will be?" he asked
his guard, with a seeming nonchalance.
Supposedly the answer was: "I suspect your left leg,
wounded at Quebec and Saratoga
in the American cause, will be cut off
and buried with proper military honors.
The other of you we shall hang."

Mingles

This boy is sleeping on concrete. Really "sleeping"
isn't accurate, it's just a duller and beaten-down

version of being awake. He's sleeping on concrete, peeing
(his first night here, before he's "processed")

in a community bucket, and breakfasting
on a sour scuffed-up apple and dry burnt toast.

Not that the orderlies who work this "holding facility"
are at fault: they're understaffed and underfunded.

Wherever she is, at a different facility his sister
doesn't have it any easier. They've been separated,

for no particular reason
except the blind moves of bureaucracy. He

chews his nails down to the blood. He screams sometimes
like a car alarm. Keep him in your mind,

he'll be returning in a while. The way
heart-breaking stories tend to do. They put on different faces,

ages, races, genders over time,
but they never depart the vicinity.

2.

On page 11 ("Celebrity News") one supernova rock star
is promoting his recent vinyard acquisition, and one

her high-end line of perfume. In rockstarspeak
it's called *diversifying the brand,* and

as I read the paper's news while the mixologist
here at Mingles stirs my drink, I think

if only we could understand the language,
we'd know treespeak for the same idea:

a tree, after all, being both the paper's pages
as they're whiffled by the Mingles ceiling fan *and,* too,

the huge names-carved-all-over-it slab
my lacquered wooden tabletop is. Diversifying

"tree." I'm reading the "human interest story"
about that boy. The traumatized one, who therefore

wets his runt-size mattress they've finally provided,
and the more they berate him—guess what happens—

the more he wets. His shame by now is so real
it's like a friend who follows him everywhere.

He thinks he'll never be outside and see a tree again.
He thinks he'll never see his own sister again. I'm also

reading about a boy—a celebrity boy, a rock star's son—
whose closest friend, a spaniel, ran away

into one of the spooky nearby canyons and was found,
next day, ripped into halves

like a honeycomb of glistening meat, by a bobcat.
Dozens of flies on the gobbets, making their wall of hum.

That boy won't sleep for days, the trip to Disneyland
won't help, nor will the new dog. So:

two boys; two disparate circumstances.
What we learn, I think, is that grief

is also busy diversifying its brand.
There's one for each of us.

3.

If the tree that's the daily paper
is news—and it is: some juicy motelarama

philander-drama; ancient Egypt divulging more
of its secrets (pottery, mud brick, "human bone chips")

into the media glare of Egypt 2021 A.D.;
the usual big-boy global saber-rattling—then the tree

that's my tabletop here at Mingles is old,
old news by now, ineptly carved

and grimed by time and lacquered-over:
tyrone luv zini; Katie 2-Face

is a btch; Dwayne T you dumass!
When Noelle the mixologist brings my drink

I ask if she knows how old, exactly, these are.
"I have no idea. But I studied

to be an arborist" [*wow*] "and this one here,
this faded one, that looks like it's underwater?..."

[she points out *DG* + *AW* in a heart]
"...was carved in the living tree. There was pith,

there was sap, behind this." When I offer the not unreasonable
caustic observation that they likely broke up

long before the tree was felled, she says, "You're wrong.
I know them, and they celebrated

their fortieth anniversary right here, just last September."
And so this is my cue to say that boy

will be released from "facilities custody" (no one knows
how mentally torqued by then but still, released) and

reunited with his sister—they fly to each other
across the sterile hallway like magnets; and the other boy,

the celebrity boy, will show up with a limo-full
of flowers at his spaniel's grave, recite a poem he's written,

take a deep revivifying breath, and move on
with his life. Solace is real, solace exists and is also

diversifying its manifold appearance
in this world. I suppose that nothing is only

one thing. Jesus came with a sword and Jesus
turned the other cheek. The gods have always

toyed with us maliciously, and then opened up a day
with so much birdsong that your heart takes wing.

The power of love is a curious thing,
Make-a one man weep, make another man sing,

sings Huey Lewis. Hey, it's "oldies night" at Mingles!
Put on one of your faces and join me here.

SHORT STORIES

Ah! The promise of an opening line!
If only the next could live up to it.

Terrible, Unfair Burdens

on our shoulders. The only Jew in the room
has to stand for all Jews. And the woman
cyberbiologist, the same. The wheelchair woman,
the same.
        As if the flu, the war, the broken
steering shaft (or covenant) (or marriage)
weren't enough, of course not, add this additional
weight mined out of the heart of a collapsing star.
It's like...
        here's a possible story
of that broken steering shaft and the wreck:
if there were two brothers, the one who lives
has to be both from then on.

A.M. Shift

The chalice on the top shelf looks
—he's seven—Harry Potterish. Vikingish. Pagan.
Even so, every Sunday morning he polishes it
for Christ, as every Sunday morning the Mass performed

at the altar, by its very repetition, lusters the faith
of the entire congregation. Ritual; what would we do
without ritual? The precinct house, on the a.m. shift:
what would they do with gourmet coffee

instead of the shitty sand-grit brew
they've bitched about every morning for years now,
forcing it down, deploring it
so regularly, it's a sacrament.

Mr. And Mrs. Music Critic

Every night of the season's tour, the symphony
repeated its program exactly: rooms of music
were constructed, filled with the furniture of the gods
to loll on and feel some rising dander of their
immortal lives...repeated this
unvaryingly, that was the talent, replicating
the masters' intent without diversion or wriggle.
The excitement, though—the real endorphin rush—
was in the cellar clubs, with coils of sweetish, lazy smoke
in the air, and a kind of laughter that jumps
from the sex-bone and then gets huskified
by the warmth of the throat; and here the music
invented itself in every fluent extension of itself,
like an amoeba, like an amoeba of deep
electric purr and willingness. Another example
—both of them thought this, each in a separate way—of how
fidelity is, so much of the time, the less attractive option.

The Problem with Mystic Wisdom

You might be raised to a "higher plane"
—that doesn't mean you belong there.

From the world of prayer, or art, or Kama Sutran hankypanky,
many dozens of examples. But I'm merely thinking

about the trees. When the flood waters sank,
there were pigs in the branches.

Second-Hand Effects

(Holiday Inn lobby, two hours)

We can tell by some of the faces that the sex
was great (their smiles want to float
out of their bodies and take their rightful place
among the constellations)
                        and also tell by other faces
who's stuck here for family sadness at the hospital
across the street.
                We don't need to be emotionally
gutted by hearing either type of those moanings:
we're experts in reading second-hand effects.
For example:
              The burning bush.
The lipstick smear. That certain bending
of light by which we recognize an exoplanet.
Sometimes in the bad old days they'd gather
by the hundreds outside of the prison's walls,
and when its lights went dim
a complicated gasp rose into the air
—it meant that the chair had been switched on.

Portrait in Three Liquid Stages

He was staring out the window, at the salt bay
I won't name. But I will say
that it's a great, convulsive expanse
of west coast water, and at the bend here,
out his window, it rises into what looks
like the back of a bucking bull. That's after
the rains. It also has its gentler
aspect, and can be smoothed out by the quieting
hands of the air like a light blue bedsheet.
What's important, though, to my portrait
of him, is how vast the water seems, and so
it's the first—the background—stage.
The window is the second: glass
is also a liquid; chemists call it,
appropriately, "slow liquid": you can see
in panes of antique glass a thickening
at the bottom, where the flow is collecting.
And he, of course, is the third stage.
He wouldn't cry; men typically don't.
But it was there, although no one could see it.

Patient

The poison was scattered about for the rats
but the calf got at it,
and in its dying was too slow
to escape the wolf. And so, just after
the system of the wolf in turn was compromised,
it died, and provided an easy feast,
a banquet,
for the rats. It took this long
and inventive way, kismet
being patient.

Needed

She was fine, oh she was *so* fine, at massaging
away the pain. It was her identity.
She loved to make it all better. If only he *were*
in pain...! And she hated herself for thinking it.

I saw the crutch, it was leaning against the corner
of the hallway, in the purple evening shadows, I could hear it
in its long neglect,
praying to be needed.

Resists

"Pieties," he writes to himself in a note
for a poem on devotional thinking.
One month later he finds it again.
"Panties," he reads; sloppy handwriting.
The flower of us
grows older, but the stem resists.
He's seventy four, and—"panties," still,
as if the Stone Age led
into the Stone Age, then into the Stone Age.

My Most Horrible Thought for Today

We forget, in the midst of the genocide,
that leukemia and embolisms don't give up
their millennial work.
We forget, as the totalitarian state increases
the reach of its iron grip,
that a foot still gets caught in a wheel's spokes,
is mangled, and needs to be cut off.
As the drought goes on, and the drought goes on,
and a fly walks nimbly across the eye
of a starving one-year-old,
the teenage daughter will curtly turn away from her mother
with a chilling look
and say an unforgivable word.

Night

The shortest distance between two points
is sunlight.

The moon triangulates
the terms of that simpler system.

Night *always* complicates;
its darkness isn't erasure

but secrecy. Weddings occur in the afternoon,
elopements in the blackness.

He was asleep. In his head: an amoeba
splitting. His Jacob, and his angel.

The grasses bend
and, cutting them, the man
bends too.

Be careful.

We become what we do.

Pane of Glass

In those days, "wan" meant "desirable":
you were someone who didn't need to work
the fields. Women kept themselves pale
by parasol, and men would purge their bodies
to an alabaster sheen by drinking
jeroboams of laxative. It's a curious concept:
so much effort taken on, to indicate

a negative condition. It's like watching
these two mimes who sweat to bear a great,
imaginary six-foot pane of glass through city sidewalks:
though their labor is immense, there's
nothing there. And also ancient Chinese royalty
who'd grow their fingernails seven inches. You could see
they weren't going to arrange their own tortoise-shell combs!

1931

They find the dog mysteriously dead:
the poor thing won't be stealing
her box of bonbons any more, or anything else,
and she freely weeps.
                               He comforts her this morning
after their night of love, and then he leaves
for work at the candy factory, where
he's recently been put in charge of painting glowing
radium decoration on the chocolates' swirls
—a raise in pay, and a steady continuing stream
of those gift assortments she likes.

Their Expert Work

Because of who we were, it was the books
that served our anger. I could hurt her,
claiming titles X and L; and she could wield
D and W as weapons. Finally, each of us had
a dolly of three contended cartons, and now
we could go on from there, dividing up
the friends; and the art; and the sky;
and the marrow we dripped out
into our separate pans, as if draining an engine;
and everything else we thought we'd shared
at one time: we took both hands to the edges
of the rootedmost, recalcitrant of things
and pulled them out of the walls until
their bloody tendrils flapped, we used our teeth
at the fastening cords, we licked the last
of the coating away and the underbody glistened.
Like those vats that are used in museums,
where the scavenger beetles do their expert work
of stripping the least left trappings of life
from the bones of a corpse—it wasn't pretty but
at the end we were clean.

The church bell tolls
and, in this valley, because of its acoustics,
the heads of lavender on the hillside
tremble, marking the great bronze rhythm,
and the bees become a gorgeous
rising curtain of gold: halted,
for the duration of the ringing,
from their apian labor. Even the top
of the nearby pond is shirred
—as if the universe is predicated upon
the laws of contagion.

The Barn and Its Shadow

In over a century, neither of them
has cancelled one of their dates.

The Joke About Stephen Hawking

Just minutes ago they were snufflingly munching
their Oreos-in-milk—and now
they're outside, killing each other

with pointed fingers, seven boys,
seven girls. *Bang. Bang.*
You're dead. Our penchant

for violence shows up even this early.
And then there's the joke about Stephen Hawking
as a child, playing outside with his friends:

Big Bang. Big Bang. A joke;
and yet it explains that
it was violence we were born from.

A Poem

They tell me the older I get the more
I look like my father—and so as I age forward
I age backward too.

When both of these directions
circle around and meet, I'll be able
to shake his posthumous hand.

He'll sell me an insurance policy.
I'll recite him a poem.
An old poem. It goes like this:

lips and tongue, larynx and lungs,
are what the skull uses
to say it's not dead

—as the skull is what the calcium uses
to say a single immediate shape
on its journey of many shapes

But the bed didn't want them in it,
didn't want them dreaming. The bed
was busy, it had its own dream:

the wood was alive in a forest again;
the feathers in the pillows were circling
around a lake for take-off.

Stories

How long is a minute? Ask him—the one
who's singing the three-year-old to sleep
with Her on his mind and doing the bills
with his wife *while She's the flame and the hook,*
and then, and only then, the makeshift bullshit story
of the week and the drive to where She awaits
in the love-nest room of the week, *with the guilt,*
to where She opens herself, *with the weight*
of duplicity, to where She ignites his breath....

How true is a fiction? Ask him—he's a science fiction
writer. He invents the planets, and their peoples,
and their foods and gods and songs and tools
and old sayings. Here's one:
On a world of two suns,
a man drags two shadows.

You woke, so you stopped dreaming.
The dream stopped: that was obvious.
And yet there are those nights

when you return in half an hour
—after fretting, counting dollars, or whatever—
and you set your head back into the dream

—set there like
a porous stone
back into the bed of a river.

Men

The club is dark, the stage is lit,
and most lit is the naked dancer
opening her tawny vee of secrets to the room
—and so, controlling the room.
There's not a single eye that doesn't arrow
straight to that accommodating

revelation. And then...another dancer

hurries into the dressing room off at the side, and
(we're evolved for this) for that two-second flash
of half-an-inch of light the door shows,
every one of us turns in a single swivel
—fooled again!—as if maybe an even greater
forbidden mystery exists there.

I know a secret about the world.
I'll tell you: *everything* is amazing.
A tree is light's way

of becoming sugar. As Jesus Christ was God's way
of becoming flesh. Our bodies are the loveliest way
Time has of knowing what brevity is.

Direction

The leaves can't argue against the storm,
or with each other. In a storm a tree
is a body of total concurring. When
the wind says *this way*...every leaf
is in agreement: *this way.* People,

however...in the Communist cell they bicker,
still, over whose devotion is purest.
In the monastery...whose love of God
most deeply sears the heart like a branded steer?
In the marriage. Certainly the marriage:

the vow says *this way,* and
her dreams keep tugging the other way.

Neighbor

She was searching in the yard—her keys,
I later found out. Since it was dark

enough to require a flashlight, yet
still dusk enough for me to see her,

that's how I see her: walking, for that moment,
an invisible dog on a leash of pure light.

Overhead,
two straggler geese:
not a vee,

an umlaut
trying to catch up
with its sentence.

Funeral Service

She took his hand on the way to a pew,
meaning it as a comfort for him

and herself too; maybe mainly herself.
He didn't want to be led

like a child; and gently uncoupled
his hand from hers. She was obviously

offended then...why did he always
act like that! He couldn't bear her annoyed look

out in public. And so it continued
like this. Yes; even in the face of death.

Tundra

The mosque is an affront to the victims of 9-11.
The mosque is a vibrant symbol of American freedoms.
Your mosque. My mosque. Mosquemosquemosque.

And what about his innocent "night with the guys"
he *deserves* after six days of labor? / Oh: you mean when
he deserts her all night and she cares for the kids alone?

For the bird, the hedge is a perfect place to lay its eggs.
For the insect, the eggs are a perfect place to inject
its larva. And then the fox comes along.

Four friends in a room watching television.
A show about the tundra.
So: four tundras.

The Mine

There was just enough truth in what she said
for him to swallow all of the smoke-and-mirrors,
all of the flimflam oil, in one great consequential gulp.
There was just enough aroma of lamb
remaining on the uncured lambskin cloak
for the poacher to slip among the flock without a fuss.
There was...well, there are so many examples. It's true
these feathered dab-marks are the brush strokes of a famous artist;
that's why this forgery hangs in the museum.
I'm talking of why friend X became convinced he should marry Y.
I'm talking of why friends Z and W voted the way they did.
We've all lived through this movie's creaky plot:
the mine was salted with just enough real gold.
Because there really are stars that dot the sky, there are astrologers.

To Every Time of Day, Its Physics

We know the sun doesn't really "rise."
We know a body is really mostly empty air.
We know so much

and so little, here
in Newtonian space: not
macro; and not micro; but the one

where I'm sitting on the porch
at dawn, my brain being charged like a battery:
the sun won't stop pouring its gold out.

LESS

It's hard to believe that all this is taking place within a book. The people must be very small.

– Yoel Hoffman, *Moods*
(tr. Peter Cole)

Small Suite

This time she's left for good
is language he can't stop stirring
obsessively and dolefully in the small cup
his attention has shrunk to become, and by
"for good" he means "for certain" and,
sadly, "permanently"
—there's nothing "good" about it.
He probably could have stopped that door
from decisively slamming, with a single word
of apology. *But he wasn't big enough for that*
is language his brain will repeat to itself
all night, sometimes accompanied by his fist
to his head, for punctuation. *One word.*
But no, not him. That's it in a nutshell,
as his aunt Dottie always said, and he can hear
the fatalistic twist with which she chirped those words.
The door. The fist. The echoing slam.
"That's it in a nutshell."

A nutshell (with a leaf raised for a sail)
serves as a two-seater boat for Bucky Bug.
In *The Little People* comic books, the inchling heroes
live in a tree stump house; and one of our shoes
(on wheels) serves them for a carriage, etc. Much
the same in *The Teenie Weenies:* their exploits
and benign camaraderie take place in a realm
where the General, tricorn-topped and epauletted,
reports on preparations for their festival

from his thimble lectern; a teapot of ours
(on wheels) is their fire engine, etc. Many
examples from my childhood, by the dozens,
and from the childhood of the species: ancient Egypt
tells of the city of mice that finally attacks
the palace of cats, and no doubt even then the tale
was built on an earlier version. This

ubiquity: why? I guess because a child
requires a population—a universe—to love
and destroy and nurture imagination
and work out problems through,
proportionate to its child-self.
A controllable space, where the child
is mommy or daddy. Or God.
Does anyone doubt the child contains
as much of tender devotion and corrosive rage
as a Valkyrie on the opera stage, or a pumped-up Navy SEAL?

*

My mother was reading me one of those stories,
Tinyland or *The Pixies*—something I'd find cloying
now, but was a pure enchantment then.
In the basement, my father

—long-term low-rung salesman
for the Metropolitan Life Insurance Company—
was seated at his thrift-shop desk
in his skivvies, in the cheap light
of a cheap lamp, trying to argue his account books
into regimental shape. He had
four mouths to feed, a family to clothe,
and every Sunday night the weight of that
descended and pressed down. Sometimes
the numbers added up just fine.

At other times an out-of-kilter
decimal point could undo him.

In 1946, ENIAC,
the Electronic Numerical Integrator and Computer,
was introduced to the public,
"a thirty-ton machine the size of a room."
Today its functions fit
in a small mole on your earlobe; maybe,
one day, a molecule. In 1951

the IBM 704 took up "about
an eighth of an acre." Today it whispers
politicians' dreams of empire
into a chip in your wrist, or a freckle, or a diatom
in your cochlea, it prints the directive
"buy now!" on a pixelated strip of your genetic code,
it burrows in your brain meat
and it breeds there like a coil of worms
if worms were the size of proteins of DNA

—as if we're puppets on strings,
except the strings are *in* us,
and we call them nerves,
or we call them microfibers
and accept them for our nerves.

I remember: miniaturization.
So twentieth century! *So* "now."
The immense (and often gorgeous)
"cathedral radio" stationed in the living rooms
of my parents' friends awoke one day

in 1961 or '62 or '63 as my
transistor radio, tidy around
as a deck of cards.
"Albie!"—my mother—
"Take that plug out of your ear! You will...NOT...
listen to that *thing* at the dinner table!"
My father

was up from the basement, having spent the weekend
tallying nightmare ranks of figures,
to purchase the very food in front of me there.
I suppose what he wanted was simply a moment
of family solace...some hint of appreciation...
and me,

Mr. Big Shot, I was owned right then
by "Telstar," the first (and only?)
top-ten pop hit that was titled
after a telecommunications satellite,
so "now" (then), and so addicting,
huge as an orbit,
snug in my ear.

When she sucks a cock
she's sucking her thumb in the cock,
the way she did when she was a child
in search of consoling. When he eats
a pussy, *really* getting into it,
he's swimming upstream, not just back
to the womb, but to the salt,
the ocean, we all emerged from
originally.
            Because the remember-part
of the mind remembers deeply, the nipple (personal)

is never completely missing from our neural
complexity-web of association.
And the Eden story (religious)
and its correlative hunter-gatherer existence
(anthropological)—those two domains
in which "we were one with the animals"
(which is true, as well,
of the feather-stage and the gill-stage
of our pre-natal development)—may say something
relevant about our being drawn to the call

of the Little People sheltering under an awning
that's a maple leaf and trading woodland gossip
with a squirrel, and of the Teenie Weenies
thriftily negotiating payment with a mole
they'd like to dig some underground
storage tunnels for them.
                    Once
it felt wrong (stickily sweet
and less than "manly" of me), this yielding
to nostalgia. All of those people out there
making a quasi-sacrament of the jingly theme song lyrics
from their childhoods' favorite t.v. shows.
But I've reached an uneasy accommodation
with Old One and his diminutive
tree stump citizens, and their beckoning.
From Guy Gavriel Kay's *The Last Light of the Sun*:

"*Heimthra* was the word used for longing:
for home, for the past,
for things to be as they once had been.
Even the gods were said to know that yearning,
from when the worlds were broken."

So in an atom there are, like, littler things,
"electrons" and "protons" and empty air and stuff
like a solar system or something. So maybe
the Earth is like an atom in some universe or something
we can't imagine. It turns out

that the idle mouthy play of precocious
eleven-year-olds and the work
of Nobel cosmologists aren't really so very

different. In that context, it makes sense
of a kind, to wonder of the Little People
—Old One, Chub, Loop, Jink and Cork—
how micro-tiny, *unfindably* micro-tiny,
would *their* gastrointestinal flora be?

"He prayeth best who loveth best
all creatures, great and small"
– Coleridge...implying the addition
of deity into the mix. The Little People,
Old One and his thumb-high cohorts
...what size is their God?
Do gods *have* "size"?
Like, maybe WE'RE God's bacteria!

They easily could have held him up
      to ridicule—*the Earth*
revolves around the Sun? The perfectly

unblemished orbs in our Good Lord's
      perfect system are streaked
and pitted? You nutso joker!

That the Vatican threatened Galileo
    with puncturing his eyes
says that in fact they took his observations

seriously enough to be a serious threat
    to the reigning order. One never knows
what the everyday ragtag population

will choose to believe; the milk goes sour
    before its time, a certain circle
inside a field refuses to spring up

greenly with the rest, and suddenly
    generations of them will swear
to "little people"—elves or gnomes—

as real creatures lurking in the scumble of shadows
    along the edges of woods. And so
that visionary heliocentric thinker

was forced to recant the entire solar system
    he'd joyfully decanted. Meanwhile,
Leeuwenhoek was alarming-delighting

his neighbors with the world's
    first looks at the dizzying
profusion of swimming paisleys

he called his "animalcules,"
    that his "seeing lenses" called up
out of spit or rotting cheese.

It's not as if I want to have lived
    then. Still...to be there!
—to be present on the cusp of when

a microbe and a planet
    were equivalent shocks to the orthodoxy;
equally a marvel.

On July 30, 2020, in an auction
of book curiosa, a one-of-a-kind example
of Matthias Buchinger's microcalligraphy
(dating from 1720-1721), achieved a hammer price
of $12,500: a truly gigantic amount

per inch, as the whole construction
is under two inches: "a wood and ivory case
in the shape of a book, containing
under glazed panels—one front, one back—
a sampling of Buchinger's mastery
at microscript." I'm looking at a photograph

of the side presenting the Ten Commandments
as if on their original stone tablets,
with red ink floral-like sprays
surrounding it for a border. Every word,
exactingly formed and readily legible.
Under two inches. "In a nutshell."
Is it meaningful (or not) that the artist,

often called "The Little Man of Nuremberg,"
was twenty-nine inches tall?
Is all that amazing enough, or should I add
(and I am) that he was born without legs
"and with stumps for arms, that ended
in fin-like appendages"—and, beyond
his gift for pen-work, he
"built highly detailed models of ships in bottles"
and drew portraits, landscapes, family trees

and coats of arms, proficiently played at least ten
musical instruments (some of his own invention),
danced the hornpipe, offered conjuring shows
(in which one trick was producing
a live bird out of an empty cup),
"and displayed his skill [*with fins!*]
as a marksman and swordsman."*
Not long after, in 1738, in Pennsylvania,

Benjamin Lay, who was "hunchbacked,
bowed, and only four feet tall"
and an adamant abolitionist Quaker
in a time when American Quakers still owned slaves,
secured a pig's bladder (filled with darkly crimson
pokeberry juice) in a Bible, and with it
burst into a crowded meetinghouse,
exhorting, in a thundering voice, "Oh
all you Negro masters...God shall shed the blood
of those persons who seek to enslave their fellow creatures!"
—at which he climactically pierced the Bible with a sword,
and to the parishioners it seemed to explode
with blood, that splattered over their heads
and good church clothes. Now *that's*
political theater! It could be

our standard metric for "stature"
should have the height requirement taken out.

[*Biographer Ricky Jay: "That he possessed one fully operative appendage is
verified" by four wives and fourteen offspring. "One of the earliest known
valentines" was a gift to one of his daughters.]

It happens this way:
She needs to return for her toiletries.
Or doesn't, really. She can buy more.
But a few of those lotions they don't even make
by now, and her skin has learned a special
intimacy with them. And this is a time of day
when he shouldn't be home.
He's home. They both stare, as startled
as deer in headlights—as *susceptible.*
And then, without preamble, somehow
he does ascend from his own self-damaging
smallness of spirit, and says a healing word.
A salve. An assuagement.
I'd be dishonest if, in the interest
of a "feel-good moment," this poem implied
the path they'll travel together now
is smooth and rose-petals strewn.
But it's indeed a path *together,* and given
who they are, and what they need, it's the best
(this wouldn't be true for everybody)
possibility, even limiting of future possibilities
though it is. Let's quote
Guy Gavriel Kay a second time:
"It happens this way.
Small things,
accidents of timing and congruence:
and then all that flows from our lives in such moments
owes its unfolding course to them."

*

But how can we care
about those two, why *should* we, when
the cyberwars of superpower enemy states are in collision,
in collusion, are counterinsurgency, cryptocurrency,
data in a data-continuum:

new war, old war, boarded storefront,
bomb blast, wealth tax, NASA, NASCAR, dealmakers,
bootieshakers, clickbait, tailgate, dolphin, endorphin,
schism, jism, socialism, bullet
through the sternum of a two-year-old,
through a generation of two-year-olds,
Hollywood, twittertumblr, Heaven and Hell and NFL,
most valued player, ozone layer,
playstation, space station, goal posts, re-posts,
surveillance state and interest rate...
                                            this
intercontinental inundation dwarfs
whatever piddly urgencies we call our lives,
it pulls on our awareness with the gravity
of a planet...
                    and yet (and this is the part
they *love* at Power-Entertainment-Mindfuck
Central Headquarters, where our up-for-grabs attention
is increasingly commodified) it will enter
into your consciousness through a gateway
sized to your neural-storage profile,
all of the dot-com, rom-com,
motherboard and fatherland
emails, shemales, save-the-whales overmuchitude
will fit in a techno-access lane
the size of your ribonucleic acid, and now, at last,
the high gods of the information economy
will whisper your commands for the day
directly into your bile, your serotonin, your glucose,
will orbit your blood, will be your personal
barcode platelet, be a Telstar
the size of a boson
keeping you transfixed with its song.

Every seven years we're completely new cells.
– the common understanding of sloughing and regenerating

In *The Incredible Shrinking Man*, the movie's hero,
having boated through a radioactive mist,

begins his special-effects one-way diminuendo
by seeing his clothes—as if it isn't him

that's changing—going baggy. Soon
he's lost in them. And soon again

he's being toyed with,
by a household cat. And after that,

the terrifying scene everybody remembers
with the spider. At the end, he exits through

the interstice-square of a window screen
as if through a temple's portal.

He's finally so infinitesimal,
he enters the infinite fabric of the universe

itself. That's counterintuitive, but
true. It may be the single greatest

spiritual moment in 1950s American film.
Surely it's your story

and mine: although we do it
one cell at a time.

My father fancied himself a man
who knew the men who knew the men
it was expedient to know. This was Chicago,
the fifties, early sixties: people with an "in"
with Mayor Daley's chief ward bosses could sometimes
catch a favor—a bone—indifferently
thrown their way. In addition to synagogue services,
my father would occasionally visit the pool halls,
stop by the local alderman's office, "rubbing,"
he'd say, "elbows with the boys."
The boys. As if he were part of a team
of insiders. In fact, my father

was too damn decent to fit in there, and
too inconsequential. When we were stopped
by a Chicago cop for accidentally running a light,
and my father offered "to buy him lunch"
in exchange for a pass on the ticket
—*that's how "the boys" always did it*—
his hands shook, slipping the twenty
out of his leatherette wallet. They
shook: *not*
cool. Though I think now it speaks
well of him—a man whose heart was open
to the confusions of feeling integrity. I only saw him

cry one time—when I was thirteen and told him
I didn't believe in God—but that doesn't mean
there weren't other occasions, or that
like anybody, like you, there wouldn't have been
interior weeping: his mother's and sister's
funerals would surely have been proof.
But enough of that. Forget it.
For now, we're going to join him

in line at the nearby bank on a December day
of floor-mop gray in the sky, with a few large
buzzsaw flakes of snow beginning to fall.
He's nervous. Ashamed. Because this month
his labors weren't sufficient: and now he needs
a loan until the first (he's practiced saying that,
"just till the first," as if it would act
as a magic talisman: it was running
humiliatingly through his head even now
as the snow outside began to adhere to ledges
and, inside, the awkward shufflings and coughs
of other waiting aspirants served as an *a capella* chorus,
"till the first, till the first").
His credit was iffy. He'd put on a tie
to formalize this abasement. *My man,*

a poolroom sharpie said yesterday, don't wooooory,
I slipped 'em the word, they're gonna treat you like a PRINCE!
Except he'd been waiting for over two hours,
watching a man with manicured nails
and a crooked skinny cigar, and a woman
in heels and a fox stole (head and paws intact),
get ushered in immediately,
as if on greased wheels. So here he is now,

here he is (maybe thinking of me),
sitting next to the neighborhood cobbler
(there were cobblers back then), who was next
to the seam-faced washerwoman
worrying the edge of her babushka, who was next
to the guy who ran the corner newspaper-peanuts kiosk
and is worrying that his noodnik son
is letting the papers get snowed on.
My father is here, with his community.
The little people.
The ones the politicians swear they care for.

Less

Drops so large they hit as silver dollars
on the street could be a devastating flood

in just an hour; however, vanishing,
as last night's downpour did, in a couple of blinks,

that rain ruins less than misty drizzle
over a week does: creeping gray rosettes

of mold along our storeroom walls are evidence
of this, and of the general idea that

sometimes more can be effected with less.

Those lavishly crazy Victorians! On the opening night
of Sydenham Park, near London,
sculptor Benjamin Waterhouse Hawkins, working with
Sir Richard Owen himself (the man who gave the world the word
dinosauria), hosted a dinner to preview (and boast of)
the vast faux-Paleozoic grounds and looming life-size
dinosaur models (some as much as thirty tons).
The invitations (written on artificial pterodactyl wings)
went out to twenty-one people, who, on arrival,
were seated (and served their first of *many* drinks)
"inside the belly of an iguanodon." And yes,
I'd like to have been there, singing
tipsily as the night came on, and that belly the size
of a banquet hall flickered with candlelight. But why

am I moved more deeply by the body
of the mummified four-month-old

from northern Lebanon, a wisp of hair
between her toes, left there unintentionally
by the grieving mother? It's catching:
writing those lines, I feel like crying;
as if there's a hair in my eye.

The hunter kills the
[bison; walrus; fill in the blank _____]
and kneels at the side of this body
still warm to his touch; and then
he pricks his arm with the Blade of Respect,
        he lessens himself
by a trickle of blood, of offering-blood,
that he lets drop onto the hide of the beast
in reverence and thanks.
                     I'm also thinking
of the fox in the trap, that gnaws itself
to freedom, one paw less now, but
alive.
      I'm also thinking
of Disney's insight: if they'd only lessen Mickey's
hands by a finger—by only a single finger
in every hand-drawn cel—the savings in paint cost
and in time would be incalculably
immense. (In the 1929 publicity drawing
by Les Clark, we can see a full
five-fingered hand as Mickey plays
his one-string mandolin.) In a way, this sacrificial
finger is what allowed the total
global Disney empire of today.

Do we believe that the meek shall inherit?
Do we believe a Goliath quakes the earth

when he smashes onto it slingshot
by a pint-size David? I can't answer those questions

for you. I do know that the dinosaurs are dead
but the birds they became are here

and flying, they evolved to have anatomically
so little in them.

But (transparency): I delight
in abundance

or anyway certain kinds of abundance.
Who *wouldn't* desire a tour
of the American Museum of Natural History's
100 elephants,

one million birds,
"600,000 fishes in jars of alcohol,"
1.6 million beetles,
the rug of forty platypus skins
("they were killed," the curator says, "by some idiot"),
the weaver bird nest—one nest!—
of 400 cubic feet.
Meanwhile, on the other coast: Renee Tourneau's
one-woman, world's-largest, collection
of souvenir thimbles by state.
Who *wouldn't* cherish this photograph
of the enormous penguin colony
of nuns, at lunch at the annual convention
of the Sisters of Holy Works.

Art Aufderheide, legendary pathologist,
has dissected over 800 mummified bodies.
Imelda Marcos's shoes.
King Solomon's wives.

Walt Whitman's breath-taking catalogues
of humanity, that seem to hold
the whole of us in their exuberance
(read "The Sleepers"). And the beautiful
excess of plaintive yearning,
battalions of Valkyries, and alternating
too-much-thunder and too-many-trumpets
in overachieving operas
(do they *really* need a brace of leopards
on gilded leashes shoehorned into the wedding scene?).
And epic poems!
The Iliad! The Divine Comedy!
Although

as soon as I say that,
Li Po rises
from the grave that any caring poet
should honor, to remind us
that the haiku also
bears the planet safely across the great celestial spheres.
He's saying

        Midnight: now the doors are locked.
           A cricket
        sings in the opera house.

Betweenish

*"We are strangely lacking in middling terms—words to
describe with some precision the middle ground
between hard and soft, near and far, big and little."*
– Bill Bryson

It's dawn: the warrior chieftan
strides from the flap of his yurt into air
still dallying coyly with the chill of the night,
and so the fresh enemy heads he carries
in either hand—from last night's raid—
are still (and extra) warm to his touch.
He sniffs; he sniffs and smiles. He can scent
new enemy heads on the wind...

                                  as

elsewhere, the monk in his solitary
eyrie on the mountain's tip—inured
by now to the chill, and even welcoming
its call to alertness—hums a mantra
that serves as a doorway
into the Sevenfold Contemplation...

                                      even

as someone—I think I'll claim
this person represents you and me—
is watching the beads of sweat form
on the kettle of tea, and looking out the window
at the pile of mulch that needs to be
dispersed throughout the garden, and idly
listening to the children's breathing
                                    here,
in what some traditions would have properly called
The Middle Way.

The Chicago brothel harlot Diamond Bertha
"who had no problem crashing a bottle of champagne
over a man's head" was requested by the madams there,
because of this conduct, to seek employment elsewhere.
This was 1910. In six months she was found
"in a New Orleans alleyway, her hands, adorned
with every bracelet and ring she owned, sliced off
at the wrists."
              That same year,
in a village in Poland that you or I might think of
as insignificant, the Virgin Mary thought
better of, and manifested her radiant
and all-benevolent self to a local shepherd girl
known for her saintly comportment, whose touch
thereafter could ease the pain
of women in difficult labor.
                 Still, somewhere
someone is mowing the grass, or smoking some grass,
or adding a touch of lemongrass to the curry.
Maybe a bill to pay
by squeezing some moneyblood
out of a dug-up moneystone.
Maybe a squabble to stroke
into quietude, a car to suds,
or a spouse's shoulder.
Maybe a little pastrami on rye.

ACKNOWLEDGMENTS

Some of these poems originally appeared in literary journals, and my deep gratitude goes to the editors of *The American Journal of Poetry; Conduit; December; The Gettysburg Review; Green Mountains Review; 32 Poems; Willow Springs.*

Mark Drew's editorial acumen receives a special tip of the hat, as does Toni Loeffler's assistance. For half a century, Christopher Howell's passionate dedication—as poet, editor, teacher—has enriched the world of poetry for all of us.

None of these poems was created using computer technology.